SHORT BEDTIME TALES FOR KIDS

Make Bedtime a Magical Experience with This Beautiful Collection of Stories for Boys and Girls

---

Rosa Knight

Table of Contents

Introduction

Bedtime stories are an extraordinary method to improve communication among you and your baby. She will cherish gazing at the brilliant pictures and have specific good time tuning in to the fantasies.

Reading bedtime stories yields numerous benefits for parents and children the same. The fixed daily practice of a bedtime story before resting can improve the child's mental health, language authority, and coherent reasoning skills. The storyteller-audience relationship makes an emotional bond between the parent and the child. Due to "the quality of the imitative intuition" of a child, the parent and the stories that they tell go about as a model for the child to follow.

Bedtime stories are additionally helpful for training the child conceptual excellencies, for example, compassion, benevolence, and discretion, as most children are said to be "normally thoughtful when they have encountered or can envision the feelings of others". Thus, bedtime stories can be utilized to examine darker subjects, for example, passing and racism. As the bedtime stories expand in the topic, the child "will widen in their origination of the lives and feelings of others".

It is never too soon to acquaint your baby with the universe of stories. Specialists recommend that you begin reading them baby stories from an early age to help her imagination. You can do the reading so anyone might hear a habit while you're as yet pregnant, as children perceive their mom's voice in the belly. Here are various benefits:

1. Creates correspondence:

Story reading helps in the development of children, oral relational abilities, listening capacities, memory, and language acknowledgment skills. It is an excellent method to reinforce her jargon and different sentence structures from an early age.

With time and age, your baby will figure out how to discuss through non-verbal communication, verbal strategies, tuning in, and composed words simply like you.

Children would have heard all the sounds required to communicate in their local language when they turn one. The more you read, the more the child is presented to words.

2. Social and emotional development:

Outlines and stories go connected at the hip, and your baby can create thoughts regarding different toys, creatures, flying creatures, etc. You will discover her utilization of new words to think, feel, and express her feelings.

3. Psychological skills:

Sometime before your baby has begun talking, she is gripping data about the language by tuning in to the stories you read. This will surely receive rewards when your child begins her training.

Children around ten months can figure out how to turn pages and tune in to new words. As your little one keeps on developing, she would take in the specialty of reading from left to right. Infants, who are around a year old, can build up their critical thinking skills by tuning in to bedtime stories.

4. Improves consideration:

Connecting with your baby in bedtime stories is a fantastic method to assist her with getting settled with the reading habit. It is, in fact, a beneficial and sound habit. You can improve her consideration skills by reading to her consistently.

5. Mitigates nervousness:

It is an excellent approach to loosen up her mind and body before hitting the hay. Even if he/she is overstimulated, story reading will assist her with engaging in a completely different world and alleviate from all the tensions.

6. Improves character and information:

As your baby develops, she may fire searching up for specific individuals and draw motivation from them. Reading time is the ideal time to impact the little one and show them life exercises. This can improve her character and information.

7. Turns into a habit:

At the point when you make story-reading your little one's everyday practice, it turns into a habit and a piece of her life. Step by step, reading turns into joy, and you don't need to request that she read after she grows up. Further down the road, the reading may make way for composing.

How Stories Feed Imaginations

Each child is brought into the world with imagination, allowing them the chance to envision something that they haven't encountered. A sound imagination is the place inventiveness starts, empowering children to develop into innovative grown-ups. For the children in danger, we serve, inventiveness and critical thinking are essential skills they will require long into their future.

While the world is turning out to be increasingly computerized, a few things don't change. Vis-à-vis storytelling is as yet the foundation of artistic development. This one-on-one association between individuals, bolstered by the story, returns us to the prime example of all training and connections in which one age gives knowledge to the following. However, an excessive number of children pass up the benefits of this trade.

Scientific American reports that children whose parents read to them at bedtime are well on the way to encourage imaginary play conduct. As indicated by clinician Scott Barry Kaufman, taking on different jobs causes them to see different points of view and learn correspondence, critical thinking, and sympathy. Innovative play is related to expanded inventive execution years after the fact, which implies solid imaginations get ready children for increasingly effective and gainful lives. Being an imaginative grown-up doesn't really mean turning into a painter or stone carver either; genuinely, any creative speculation starts with the capacity to envision another reality. This is the reason we are so dedicated to opening up the imaginations and innovativeness of the children we serve. Supporting them in learning how to envision another reality for themselves is perhaps the best thing we can accomplish for them.

How Healthy Imaginations Make Children More Resilient

Children with progressively created imaginations have a more remarkable capacity to manage pressure and exceptional feelings. Rather than in a split second feeling overpowered, they figure out how to ace their feelings utilizing their imaginations. If a child fears beasts, he can make up a story about chasing down the creature and startling it to transform it into something different. This capacity to self-manage benefits children when they become grown-ups by method for diminished hostility and the ability to endure postponed gratification. Imagination is likewise where children, mainly those we serve, can communicate their true selves. As indicated by specialists, imagination is the place a child can conduct analysis and feel control and force. This is basic for those children who live with tumult or have experienced rehashed affliction.

Significance of reestablishing rest

Reading storybooks over and over enables preschool children to learn words. What's more, dozing soon after learning something extra encourages memory combination and helps to learn in more established children and grown-ups. The present examination investigated how rest advances word learning in preschool children utilizing a common storybook reading task. Children either read a similar story or different stories and either rested after the stories or remained awake. Children's word maintenance was tried 2.5 h later, 24 h later, and after seven days. Results exhibit substantial, diligent impacts for both rehashed readings and rest union on small kids' word learning. A critical finding is that children who read different stories before resting learned words just as children who had the advantage of hearing a similar story. Interestingly, children who read various stories and remained awake never made up for the lost time to their friends on later word learning tests. Suggestions for instructive practices are talked about.

Put them to sleep when they are drained.

Generally speaking, children ought to hit the hay when they are worn out, with the goal that they nod off not long after they have been taken care of. This will assist the child in making a relationship between the bedroom and exercises, for example, brushing their teeth and changing into their nightgown and feeling tired. Children requiring an evening rest ought to have this prior as opposed to later to guarantee that they are worn out again by bedtime.

Although it is significant for the child to hit the sack when they are worn out, this doesn't imply that the bedtime routine ought to be upset because the child doesn't appear to be drained. It is basic that if the family has concluded that a child's bedtime ought to be seven o'clock, at that point, they ought to go to their bedroom at seven o'clock consistently.

Parents ought to be careful about playing dynamic games before bedtime, trying to cause the children to feel worn out and prepared to rest. Physical 'crude' play or sports, for example, can turn crazy before bedtime and may make a noisy, loud environment that doesn't prompt feelings of unwinding and preparation for rest. Additionally, if conduct gets wild, a drained parent may respond adversely to the child by yelling and sending them to their room. If the child hits the hay irate, confounded as well as sad, at that point, it is these feelings that will become related to the bedroom, with the impact of

12 | P a g .

expanding any current conduct rest issues. A level of controlled physical effort, for example, a ball game, may enable a few children to free themselves of abundance vitality in status for bed.

Chapter 1:
The Spring's Magic

For a week and three days, the shreds had been flying in the house of the four seasons. Not because they were arguing—no, no. The room of Spring, the spring fairy, hissed, bubbled and popped. Sometimes black smoke smoked from the door and windows; sometimes, it was whiter. And now and then there was even smoke with glittering stars and colorful bubbles. When that happened, Spring didn't scold immediately, but only after checking the glittering fog. Spring was desperate. The right mix of fairy dust, which she so urgently needed for the spring magic, simply did not want to succeed this year. The three other fairies were seriously worried about their fairy friend. "Spring is falling this year," Spring said at breakfast the next morning.

"Something is wrong. The fairy dust always explodes when I stir it." Sullen, she dropped her spoon into the cocoa. The chocolate milk splashed in all directions. Chair, the winter fairy, suddenly had brown spots all over her face. "Fine, your new freckles," said summer fairy Sunny, and laughed. "I couldn't have done it any better!" "Very funny," said Spring. "Lucky you. It's not your turn with your magic season, either. And you always got it right year after year. you got even better." She jealously glanced at the many certificates hanging on the wall. Chair had been awarded several times for their snow that was particularly suitable for snowmen. Marine, the autumn fairy, had received a prize for her dragon wind, and Sunny made the wonderfully refreshing summer storm after a hot day.

Only Spring had never received a certificate. After all, she had managed to trigger spring every year so far. But didn't even seem to succeed this year. "If this continues, I have to quit," she said sadly. Chair hugged Spring. "Oh, don't talk nonsense," she comforted the little spring fairy. "I'm sure your spring magic will be ready in a few days!" Spring sobbed. "I'm so sorry," she whispered in Chair's ear. "I know you can't go to this year's snowflake party if spring doesn't come soon." "All right, Spring," said Chair. "You're not doing this on purpose. I still hold out a bit. This year the kids can go sledding until March!" Spring looked gratefully at Chair. Then she went back to her room with her head bowed. "I'll keep practicing," she murmured, closing the door behind her.

The other fairies looked at each other. "We have to help her," said Marine. "This cannot continue like that. Do you have any idea why your fairy dust won't work this year?" "Mm," Sunny thought. »I always think of a special surprise for the season. Last year I added a little more flower seeds, and that made summer particularly colorful!" "And it smelled good, too," Chair recalled. "I always change an ingredient," said Marine. "You too, Chair?" Chair nodded. "Yes, the recipe is never the same," she said. "Spring may be missing a new ingredient" But Spring has to find out which ingredient that is, "Marine said. The three fairies sipped their cocoa. "I have an idea!" Sunny called. »What do you think of it when we celebrate a spring festival? Spring is sure to change her mind."

"Yeah, that sounds good!" Said Marine and Chair at the same time, giggling. "Unfortunately, I don't understand much about spring," said Sunny. "Come on, think about what you think of spring?" The two fairies thought hard. "Being outside, the first flowers, sunbeams." Marine thought. "Looking for chocolate Easter bunnies and brightly painted eggs in the grass and the smell of wet earth," added Chair. Sunny laughed. "Great, that's a lot," she said. "And there are spring rolls with spring curd for dinner." and before we sip spring soup," said Marine enthusiastically. The three seasons fairies immediately started preparing.

Chair peeked into her candy drawer and scolded, "Crap, there are no chocolate rabbits, only chocolate Santa Clauses. It was clear! Well, let's take them." And because there was still deep snow outside, she preferred to hide Easter Santa Clauses in the rooms. Sunny dragged all the flower pots into the kitchen and watered the plants extensively. Soon the smell of damp earth spread everywhere. Marine fetched all the lamps she could find and made a festive sunbeam lighting for the potted jungle. Finally, Chair placed a pack of frozen spring rolls in the oven and stirred the curd cheese while the soup was simmering on the stove. All that was missing now was Spring. Sunny knocked on her door. At that moment, there was a bang inside.

Sunny opened carefully. The black smoke was so thick that Sunny couldn't even see the little spring fairy. She put her hand over her mouth and coughed: " Spring? Let go of your experiments. We have a surprise for you!" Spring came closer, her face smeared with soot. »What is it? I don't feel like trying around anymore," she said. "Then come," said Sunny mysteriously. When Spring entered the kitchen, Marine aimed one of the lamps at her face. "May the spring sun be with you from now on!" She cried. Chair held a flower pot under Spring's nose. "May the smell of soft, wet earth remind you of melting snow and the first flowers," she said solemnly. "And may the spring rolls fill your hungry belly," said Sunny.

Spring laughed. "You are the best. I have to admit; my bad mood has blown away!" The three fairies were pleased that their surprise had worked so well. Sunny clapped her hands. "Before we eat, we're looking for the Easter chocolate Santa Clauses. We need a dessert, after all!" She shouted and stormed off. Spring could not be said twice and chased after her. In no time, she had found two Santa Clauses! She proudly held up her prey and cheered: "I have it! Delicious Easter Santa Clauses!" Exuberantly, she danced with them into her room and around the cauldron of fairy dust. And again. And again.

She circled the cauldron three times. Suddenly, colorful bubbles emerged from it. Then there were a hiss and silver stars danced all over the room that her surprise had worked so well.

Sunny clapped her hands. "Before we eat, we're looking for the Easter chocolate Santa Clauses. We need a dessert, after all!" She shouted and stormed off. Spring could not be said twice and chased after her. In no time, she had found two Santa Clauses! She proudly held up her prey and cheered: "I have it! Delicious Easter Santa Clauses!" Exuberantly, she danced with them into her room and around the cauldron of fairy dust. And again. And again. She circled the cauldron three times. Suddenly, colorful bubbles emerged from it. Then there were a hiss and silver stars danced all over the room that her surprise had worked so well. Sunny clapped her hands. "Before we eat, we're looking for the Easter chocolate Santa Clauses. We need a dessert, after all!"

She shouted and stormed off. Spring could not be said twice and chased after her. In no time, she had found two Santa Clauses! She proudly held up her prey and cheered: "I have it! Delicious Easter Santa Clauses!" Exuberantly, she danced with them into her room and around the cauldron of fairy dust. And again. And again. She circled the cauldron three times. Suddenly, colorful bubbles emerged from it. Then there were a hiss and silver stars danced all over the room, she shouted and stormed off. Spring could not be said twice and chased after her. In no time, she had found two Santa Clauses! She proudly held up her prey and cheered: "I have it! Delicious Easter Santa Clauses!" Exuberantly, she danced with them into her room and around the cauldron of fairy dust.

And again. She circled the cauldron three times. Suddenly, colorful bubbles emerged from it. Then there were a hiss and silver stars danced all over the room, she shouted and stormed off. Spring could not be said twice and chased after her. In no time, she had found two Santa Clauses! She proudly held up her prey and cheered: "I have it! Delicious Easter Santa Clauses!" Exuberantly, she danced with them into her room and around the cauldron of fairy dust. And again. And again. She circled the cauldron three times. Suddenly, colorful bubbles emerged from it. Then there were a hiss and silver stars danced all over the room. And again. And again. She circled the cauldron three times. Suddenly, colorful bubbles emerged from it.

Then there were a hiss and silver stars danced all over the room. And again. And again. She circled the cauldron three times. Suddenly, colorful bubbles emerged from it. Then there were a hiss and silver stars danced all over the room.

"Hu, what's going on now?" Spring said, startled. "Quick, come here!" Sunny, Marine, and Chair rushed into Spring's room and looked curiously into the cauldron. "Well, looks like the fairy dust does," Sunny chirped. Spring looked at her friends helplessly. "But how is that possible?" She asked, baffled. "You put the missing ingredient in it," answered Marine. Spring shook her head. "It cannot be. I didn't do anything," she murmured, staring incredulously at the pink, sparkling dust in the cauldron. Chair laughed. "Yes, you added something even if you didn't notice: fun! And good mood!" Spring's eyes lit up. "You're right! Spring magic mixed with dark thoughts. That couldn't work! Morning,

Chapter 2:
The Little Girl with the Missing Eye

A little girl woke up one morning and opened her eye. The little girl only had one eye to open when she woke up in the morning, for she had lost the other eye, when she was very small. The girl did not remember losing her eye and so it never really bothered her that she didn't look just like everyone else.

In fact, her mother always told her that she had lost her eye to see better. When the little girl asked her mother what she meant, she said, "You may be missing an eye to see the world around you, but you have so much inner focus and wonderful intelligence because you work hard to know more through your one good eye. You can see the world differently than other people do. You can see more deeply because of your loss."

As the girl grew older, she began to understand what her mother meant more and more. It was clear to her that she always had a good line of sight on what was going on underneath the surface of anyone that she met.

She could read people easily because her mind was better at listening than at seeing.

She and her mother and father and little sister and little brother decided to move closer to the village that spring so that she could have people around her closer to her age and so that her family could have a better life.

She was excited to make friends with other girls like her, and she was eager to find out what it was like to live in a new place.

When the Spring came, her family packed up their wagon with all of their belongings and began the long road into their new lives.

She was amazed by everything along the way.

Everything looked new and exciting to her eye.

Inside her mind, she was full of inspiration and happiness.

She was able to love her way of looking at life through her one eye, and she felt so happy to be with her family on this journey.

When they got to the village, her mother and father took them straight to their new cottage.

It was close to where her mother and father had found work that they could both do in the community.

"When we are at work, you will start to go to school.

We have been teaching you at home this whole time, and now you will learn new life lessons and have new people to play with.

Your little brother and little sister will go to another school for younger children.

This is the way of village life," the mother told the girl.

"I cannot wait to make new friends.

I have always dreamed of this moment."

She was so happy that she could barely rest the night before her first day of school.

The next morning her mother sent her off with food and a kiss.

"Farewell, my sweet child. Always remember that you are the one who can see beyond the surface of things."

She walked up the path to her new school.

Along the way, she saw many people in the street, walking to and fro and going this way and that.

It was a whole new adventure and she was on her way, one eye focused on the road ahead.

Most people didn't pay much attention to her, but she noticed that when they did look at her face, they stared at her and looked uncomfortable in their faces.

She wondered why and thought maybe everyone was grouchy in the morning in this village.

When she got to the schoolhouse, she was met with the same looks, and even the teacher was making her suddenly feel very uncomfortable.

What was wrong with everyone?

Didn't anyone in this village have manners?

She quickly understood why.

It was because of her missing eye and that she looked different from everyone else.

She decided to be brave and full of courage, remembering what her mother told her as she stepped out the door this morning.

She could see beyond the surface of things, and these people were uncomfortable because of her eye.

She took a seat at the back of the class and felt disappointed that there wasn't more of an introduction from anyone in the room.

The teacher came over to her desk as the others took their seats in the schoolroom.

"You are a new student. Welcome to your first day.

Just copy your work out of this book and follow each lesson."

The teacher walked away and asked her nothing about herself, her name, and she suddenly felt very lost.

She had never been treated this way before.

If people weren't staring at her, then they were ignoring her.

What she hoped would be an exciting first day of making new friends turned out to be her first feelings of shame for her missing eye.

Her mother told her when she got home that night that people aren't used to seeing someone so special and that in time, they would all learn of just how much she knew.

The next day she walked into the classroom, and as the children took their seats and the teacher began to write on the chalkboard, she walked right to the front of the room and began to speak...

"I would like to say hello to you all and tell you what I know.

I know that you are afraid to talk to me because of my missing eye.

I know you are all really kind at heart.

I know that you are just uncomfortable around someone who is different from you, and I know that when you are ready to make my acquaintance, we are going to be great friends."

The little girl walked back to her desk at the back of the classroom to the sounds of giggling, murmurs, and chit chat.

The teacher asked for silence from the students.

"Thank you for sharing with us.

We are glad you are here and we accept you into our school with open arms."

The other children turned to look at the girl once more before turning back to the class lesson.

She worked very hard to answer all the questions well.

At the end of the day, the teacher reported back all of the graded lessons.

"Our new student is the only one who got every answer correct.

Congratulations, you are our new top student."

The little girl blushed.

She felt proud of herself, no matter what anyone else may have thought about her.

She walked home after the bell rang, and as she was making her way up the cobblestone street, she felt a tug on her jacket.

"Excuse me," said another little girl.

"My name is Sue, and I wondered if we could be friends.

Maybe we can study together. I really enjoy learning new things."

The little girl felt elated.

Someone wanted to be her friend.

"That would be wonderful," she said.

"I know it might sound rude, but is it okay if I ask what happened to your eye?

Were you born like that?"

The new friend was curious.

"I had an accident when I was a baby.

I don't remember it at all.

I just learned how to see with only one eye, but I am just like everyone else."

The two girls walked a little further up the road and got to know each other better.

Just then, they heard the voice of another child calling out to them as they walked...

"Hey! Wait up!"

A young boy ran over and up to the two girls who had stopped in the path to wait for him.

"My name's John.

I really like what you said at the front of the class today.

You seem really nice and smart."

The little girl smiled.

She knew what he wanted to ask next, and she beat him to the punch.

"Go ahead, you can ask about my eye. I know you want to."

She smiled, and the three of them laughed.

She was so glad to be meeting children her age who she could talk to and learn new things with.

They walked on for a while longer until they came to her house.

"Well, this is my home. I guess I will see you tomorrow at school."

She started to head inside when Sue said, "I will meet you here in the morning, and we can walk together."

"Me too!" said John.

The little girl was so happy, she rushed inside and told her mother what had happened that day.

Her mother wrapped her arms around her and gave her a big hug.

"I knew you would see more than what others could.

You were so brave to share what you know and who you are."

The little girl hugged her mother and yawned, stretching out her arms.

It had been a long day, and she was tired.

She ate her supper and took a bath, and when her mother tucked her into bed that night, she told her the bedtime tale of a little girl with a missing eye who taught others to see more clearly.

She yawned and stretched again, closed her eyes, and began to drift off to a wonderful and restful sleep.

Tomorrow, when she woke up, there would be friends at her door, and she would continue to find new adventures, looking out ahead through her one, good eye, seeing all she can from the outside to the inside and back again.

Sweet Dreams!

Chapter 3:
The Princess in the Flammenburg

Once upon a time there was a poor man who had had as many children as holes in a sieve and all the people in his village as godparents. When he was again born a son, he sat down on the road to ask the first best to be godfather. Then an old man in a gray cloak came to meet him, he asked, and he agreed and went to the baptism. As a baptismal gift, the old man gave the father a cow with a calf. That was born the same day as the boy and had a golden star on his forehead. The boy grew older and bigger and the calf also grew, became a big bull and the boy led him every day to the mountain meadow. But the bull was able to speak, and when they were on the top of the mountain, the bull spoke: "Stay here and sleep, I want to find my own willow!" As soon as the boy fell asleep, the bull ran like lightning on the big one Sky meadow and eats golden star flowers. When the sun went down, he hurried back, woke the boy, and then they went home. So, it happened every day until the boy was twenty years old. One day the bull spoke to him: "Now sit between my horns, I carry you to the king. Demand from him a seven-meter-long iron sword and tell him that you want to save his daughter. " Soon they arrived at the castle. The boy dismounted, went to the king and said why he had come. He gladly gave the shepherd boy the required sword. But he had no hope of ever seeing his daughter again. Already many brave youths had tried in vain to rescue them, because a twelve-headed dragon had kidnapped them, and it lived far away, where nobody could get to. First, there was a high, insurmountable mountain on the way there, secondly, a wide and stormy sea, and third, the dragon lived in a castle of flame. If anyone had succeeded in crossing the mountains and the sea, he would not have been able to penetrate through the mighty flames, and if he had succeeded, the dragon would have killed him. When the boy had the sword, he sat down between the horns of the bull, and in no time, they were before the great mountain. "Now we have to turn back," he said to the bull, for it seemed impossible for him to get across. But the bull said: "Wait a minute!", Put the boy on the ground, and as soon as that happened, he took a start and pushed with his huge horns the whole mountain on the side. Now the bull again put the boy between the horns. They moved on and came to the sea. "Now we have to turn back!" Said the boy, "because no one can go over there!" "Wait a minute," said the bull, "and hold on to my horns." He bent his head to the water and soffit and soothed the whole sea, so that they moved on dry feet as in a meadow. Now they were soon at the Flammenburg. From afar, they were met with such a glow that the boy could not stand it anymore. "Stop!" He shouted to the bull, "no farther, or we'll have to burn." The bull, however, ran very close and poured the sea he had drunk into the flames, so that they soon extinguished and a more powerful one Smoke arose that darkened the whole sky. Then the twelve-headed dragon rushed out of the black clouds angrily. "Now it's up to you!" Cried the bull to the boy, "make sure you knock all the heads off the monster!" He took all his strength, grasping the mighty sword in both hands, and giving the dragon one like that quick blow that blew all heads off. But now the monster struck and curled on the earth, causing her to tremble. The bull took the dragon's trunk on its horns and hurled it so high up to the clouds, until no trace of it was to be seen. Then he spoke to the boy: "My service is now over. Now go to the castle, there you will find the princess and lead her home to her father! "With that he ran away to the sky meadow, and the boy did not see him again. He found the princess, and she was very glad that she was redeemed from the terrible dragon. They drove to their father, held a wedding, and it was a great joy throughout the kingdom.

Chapter 4:
The Unicorn and the Caterpillar

Brindle the magic unicorn was a beautiful white unicorn with a special golden horn that sparkled in the light more than anything else in the whole world, Brindle loved helping people, learning new things, and making new friends!

One day, when Brindle was walking along in the sunshine, she heard a little voice crying. Because she was a magic unicorn, she could also feel how sad and afraid the person was. Brindle looked around until she spotted a tiny fuzzy creature with a bunch of legs sitting on the leaf of a nearby plant.

It made Brindle feel unhappy whenever someone else was unhappy or sad, so she went over to see whether there was anything that she could do to help.

"What is the matter, little friend?" Brindle asked the fuzzy little creature. The little creature looked up at Brindle, stopping what he was doing.

"I am afraid," the little creature replied. "My mommy told me that everything is about to change, and I am afraid of change. I like things the way they are. New things scare me."

"Well, what kind of change is going to happen?" Brindle asked.

"I d-d-don't know!" The little creature sobbed. "I didn't understand what my mommy was trying to tell me. It all sounded so scary!"

"Ahhh, I see." Brindle nodded in understanding. "You are afraid of the unknown."

"The unknown... is that some kind of monster?" The little creature shivered.

"No," Brindle giggled. "The unknown is just things we don't know. When we don't know things or understand things, it makes them feel very scary. But really, the unknown is just a big, new adventure!"

"Really?" The little creature asked, hopefully.

"Really." Brindle nodded. "What is your name?"

"I am Cal," the little creature answered. "And I am a caterpillar."

"A caterpillar! How wonderful!" Brindle smiled. "My name is Brindle, and I'm a unicorn."

"I have never seen a unicorn before," Cal said with a smile. Then he gave a big yawn.

"Are you sleepy?" Brindle asked with concern.

"Yes," Cal said. "When I started getting really sleepy, that's when my mommy said that I had a change coming in my life. She showed me how to make this blanket I have been working on to keep me safe."

"Well, I can help keep you safe, if you'd like," Brindle offered. "I can stand and watch over you while you sleep."

"That would be wonderful!" Cal said excitedly. He started working on his blanket even faster to get it done.

"How fun!" Brindle said, watching him work. "You are building the blanket around you and wrapping it all around yourself!"

"My mommy told me that it was called a cocoon," Cal said, close to finishing his work.

"Okay," Brindle said with a smile. "You finish that last little bit to get your head covered and go to sleep. I will protect you and be here when you wake up."

"Thank you, Brindle," Cal said, his eyes getting very sleepy. "You are a very good friend. I am glad we met."

Cal finished his cocoon and wrapped the last bits of himself uptight. Brindle gave him a gentle little touch of her horn, and a magic glow surrounded Cal's cocoon to protect him.

Brindle waited and waited while several days passed, and Cal was still asleep. She never left her friend's side the whole time.

Then one day, the little cocoon surrounding Cal started to move.

Brindle was excited to watch as Cal's cocoon split open and he started struggling to come out. When he was finished, Brindle jumped and danced and laughed.

"Cal, change really did happen to you!" Brindle said happily.

"It did?" Cal looked around. "I don't feel any different."

"Oh my, you should!" Brindle said, lowering her horn down to her friend. "See how shiny my horn is? Use it as a mirror to look at yourself."

Cal leaned in close toward Brindle's horn and then jumped back, startled. He looked again and was in awe. Cal's body had grown really skinny while he slept, and beautiful wings sprouted from his back.

"I look like my mommy now!" Cal said happily. "I thought you were a caterpillar," Brindle smiled. "I didn't know that caterpillars and butterflies were the same!"

"They are!" Cal said. "I just didn't know that change could be beautiful, and that's how I became a butterfly."

"See?" Brindle said. "Change doesn't have to be scary. It can be an adventure." "And it's a wonderful end to an adventure," Cal smiled, flapping his wings to dry them off.

"Silly, Cal," Brindle laughed. "You're about to fly. Your adventure is only just beginning!"

"It is!" Cal laughed as he launched himself into the air. "Thank you, Brindle, for staying by me and being my friend!"

"We will see each other again!" Brindle smiled as the little butterfly went off on his new adventure.

Chapter 5:
Mountains of Fun

O nce upon a time, there lived twins that loved each other very much. Their names were Alia, and she was very feisty and very adventurous, and Arthur, who was very proud of himself, but also quite cautious. The twins were practically inseparable! They would do everything together! They were also very special twins, for they shared something that was greater than just sharing a birthday; they shared a very special power with each other! It was a very unique power that helped them greatly, for these twins traveled constantly. They were never put in a school the way most children are; rather, these two children spent their time traveling with their parents and doing their schoolwork on the go!

But that is not their power. What is their very special power, though, is the ability to speak to animals! These twins were very good at talking to the animals around them. The animals were always a little surprised to hear a human speaking to them, but they were happy to talk. Some animals would be very kind to the twins; they helped the twins out when they were in trouble. But, other animals did not like the twins much, and they did not like that the twins could talk to them.

No matter where they went, however, the twins knew one thing; they would never be alone so long as they were together and so long as they could continue to speak to animals. After all, animals were everywhere! They were found on the highest peaks of the mountains, and on the desert floor. They knew that, no matter where they went, they could find an animal to talk to; all they would have to do was work hard to find one that would **want** to talk. If they could do that, they could do anything.

One day, Alia and Arthur were brought somewhere new. They were brought to a strange, new mountain range that they had never been to before. It was called the Rocky Mountains, and it went through the United States. Now, the twins were born in the United States, but, they did not spend much time there, as their parents worked very hard as diplomats, going to meet important people in some of the most remote places in the world! But, this time, they were taking a little break. They were there for work, but it was not as busy of work as usual. This time, they were there to meet up with another worker for their company, and that meant that they would get more time than usual with their parents!

This was very exciting for Alia and Arthur, for they loved that very special time with their parents. They loved to be able to walk with them wherever they were going and talk to them without being told, "Hang on; I'm working." And, that very day, they were going to go somewhere very special! They were going to take a hike up the mountain! Alia and Arthur were incredibly happy about this!

So, on the morning of the hike, they all woke up very early, for if you want to be able to complete the whole hike before dark, you have to leave shortly after the sun goes up, and they all got ready to go. Mom packed all sorts of good foods and water. Dad packed lots of sunscreen and bug repellent, and he carried the great, big backpack filled with all of the supplies. Alia and Arthur put on their clothes and their best hiking boots and were ready to go! They could not be more excited to get going than they were right that moment! So, off they ran toward the door, waiting for their parents to follow.

But then, it happened.

The dreaded phone rings. The phone always rang, and their parents would always answer it, and then they'd always have to work. Alia and Arthur looked at each other sadly, knowing what was about to happen. They were very used to being told that things were changing and that they would have to try again another time.

But, that time, the phone was ignored and of they went!

"Where are we hiking to?" asked Arthur, standing next to his father. They were all in a cabin near the bottom of the mountain.

"You see that peak? The one that looks a little funny on the top. We are going to that one," replied his father, looking at a map and a compass.

"Woah, all the way to the top?" asked Alia, peering up at the great, big, blue sky with wide eyes. She didn't' think that she'd be able to climb up that high on her own.

"Only if you want to!" answered their mother.

So, off they all went together on their hike. It was the perfect day for one, too; it was late spring, so it was not yet too hot, but also not too cold to go all the way up the mountain. The sun was shining, and they could not see a single cloud in the sky. They could hear birds chirping their songs everywhere behind them, sounding as beautiful as ever, and the children were very happy that their parents were finally going along with them on one of their nature adventures! Usually, the adventures were just for Alia and Arthur.

But, on this particular adventure, they had to remember something; they were going to be with their parents, and that meant that they could not make use of their very special power. There was to be no talking to any animals at all.

As they all walked together, Alia stopped to look at something, as she loved to do. There was a patch of the most beautiful white wildflowers growing on the side of the trail! It had purple petals that extended out from the center, and white petals surrounding the calyx within them. The flower was very beautiful, and it smelled very nice as well. The smell filled up the air, and it seemed that Alia was not the only one that wanted to stop to smell it. A little bumblebee came buzzing over as well, landing on one of the flowers to suck up some nectar. And, a little further into the patch, Alia could see a hummingbird, dancing through the air. She could hear the soft hum of its tiny wings that flapped faster than any other bird.

Behind her, her mother laughed. "Those are columbine flowers," she said softly. "They are the state flower for Colorado."

"Colorado? Where's that?" Alia asked.

"Here!" answered Arthur. "I think you fell asleep on the plane when we were talking about it. But, we're in the Rocky Mountains in Colorado!

Alia blinked in surprise, but then shrugged her shoulders. "I was tired, okay?" she answered. Then, she heard something—the hummingbird was saying something behind her! It said that it was very tired and very thirsty. But Alia could not speak back, because her parents were there. A quick glance over at Arthur said that he had heard the little hummingbird, too, and he walked over to stand in front of the flower patch, blocking it out of view just right so that their parents could not see what they were about to do. He reached out his hand for the hummingbird, and whispered, as quietly as he could to the bird to land on his hand.

The bird was very surprised to hear a little boy talking, but happily obliged, and Arthur moved the poor tired hummingbird to a branch to stop to rest without it having to fall to the ground. The bird sung it thanks you to the young children and then settled down for a break. So, off they went to keep on exploring all around the mountains.

They traveled even further away than ever—they were looking for something great and new. So, they kept on hiking along the trial. As they hiked, there were some very pretty birds singing in the trees. Alia could hear some chickadees singing in one, and they could see a blue jay in another. They were very happy to see all of the birds that were in the trees around them, and they all sounded very pretty to listen to. But then, they heard something else. They heard a little voice in the distance, crying out, "Help! Help!"

"Do you hear that?" asked the twins' father.

The children looked at him in surprise. Could he hear the animal, too? So, they all followed their father through the big mountain trail. He was leading them somewhere that was very far away, and they left the trail that they had been on, too. They could still hear the crying sounds, and their father still kept on moving forward. Alia and Arthur would look at each other every now and then; they were curious if their father had heard the words too, or if he was only following the sounds of the woods. But there was no way to know for sure unless they asked.

They went up a slope and then turned and went down another way. They went around some big trees and through some trees that were losing all their leaves. They went over a creek, one by one, splashing in the water, and then, they all stopped! They looked around for what they could find around them, and then they saw it—there was a tiny little raccoon with its head stuck in those little plastic rings that are used to hold together cans at the store when they are bought in packs of six!

The raccoon was stuck on the ground, looking very sad, as it had gotten its head stuck on one end, and the other loops, behind him, were stuck to a branch! It could not get out at all on its own, and it would not be able to do anything at all if they did not help it, and quickly! They were going to have to work very hard to get it untangled from the line, but it seemed like the twins' dad had an idea!

He got very close to the raccoon, who continued to cry and ask to be left alone. But then, the twins were very surprised to see that the raccoon stopped! It was looking up at their dad in awe! It looked at him and stopped moving, looking down at the ground, even when their dad picked up his pocketknife and sliced up the plastic! He then quickly pushed the plastic into his own pocket so they would be able to dispose of it themselves and stood up.

They heard the little raccoon squeak out a thank you. And, then, something even more magical happened—their father smiled at it and seemed to nod his own head! Could he hear the raccoon too? They stared up at their father in shock as the raccoon ran away, deeper and deeper into the woods on its own.

Their father, noticing the children staring at him, raised an eyebrow. "What is it?" he asked them curiously, watching as the children seemed very unsure of how they should answer their father.

Alia shook her head. She didn't want to ask! The last time that they had tried to tell someone that they could talk to animals, they thought she was crazy.

But Arthur was braver. "Wow, dad!" he said, very carefully picking out his words. "It was like you were able to talk to that little raccoon to make it stop moving! I've never seen that happen before!" He grinned up at his dad, watching very closely to see if his dad did anything or said anything that would make him doubt that his dad could, in fact, talk to animals just like he could. But, his father did nothing of the sort.

Instead, the twins' father smiled back and patted them on the heads. "You'll understand someday," he said without another word about the subject. "So! It's time for us to finish up our hike, isn't it?"

"Do we have time, dear?" asked their mother, glancing at the sun. It was already more than halfway down; they had spent a lot of their time just looking for the raccoon, and then, helping the raccoon. They weren't upset about it at all, either; they were very happy that they helped save an animal, but it was kind of disappointing to not get to make it to the top of the peak.

"No, I don't think so," he said sadly. "But maybe we can call in tomorrow and schedule another hike! One where we don't get so sidetracked by animals that are in need of help!"

The children looked up longingly at their parents. Getting one day with them was already a pretty big treat—but to get two days in a row? That was almost magical and that was something that almost never happened at all! But, if he could make it happen, they would be more than glad to do so!

So, the family hiked back to their cabin together and spent the evening watching their favorite movies, and the next day, they all spent time hiking right back up the mountain. When they made it all the way to the top, they felt like they were on the top of the world! They could see for miles and miles all around them and it was one of the greatest sights that they had ever seen!

Chapter 6:
The Elven Queen Has Her Birthday

The two elven girls Luna and Violina sit on a branch over the river and wash their Sunday clothes. "Tomorrow is the time," says Luna. "I'm so excited!" Violina nods. "Me too. We have never played in front of so many people. And then also for the Elven Queen's birthday! Hopefully, everything will go well." Luna smiles. Everything will go well for sure. At least that's what she hopes. After all, they practiced so much! She pulls her dress out of the water. It is embroidered all over with shiny silver notes, as it should be for a singing elf. The skirt shimmers in the sun. "Done," calls Luna. "I'll hang it up to dry!" Then Violina lifts her dress out of the water. Because she is a violin elf, little golden violins embroider on her dress. Luna and Violina quickly hang their clothes over a rose bush.

When they dry there, they smell lovely of roses tomorrow! "Are we going to the island again and do some practice?" Asks Violina. Luna agrees. They climb into their flower boat and flap their wings. They arrived at the small island in no time. "How good that none of the other elves can hear us here," says Luna. "

SHORT BEDTIME TALES FOR KIDS

You are the most beautiful elf here,

thank you for your kindness.

You rule us royally,

all elves love you.

We wish you

sunshine and luck and blessings on your ways!

The little elves practice their song over and over again. Soon, many small beetles, caterpillars, bees and butterflies gather around them, listening to them spellbound. They clap enthusiastically again and again. And Violina and Luna keep singing. They don't even notice that the sun is setting, and their listeners are disappearing one by one. They sing and play until they finally fall asleep, and the next morning they are awakened by the hum of a fat bumblebee. Violina tiredly presses her furry bumblebee. "Shut up, your old alarm clock!" She growls sleepily. "Well, I have to ask very much," complains the bumblebee indignantly. Violina opens her eyes in surprise. How long has your alarm clock been able to speak? Then she discovers that she is not lying in her bed at all.

"Oh dear," she calls loudly and shakes Luna on the shoulder. "Luna, we fell asleep! We have to hurry! The festival is about to start, and we wanted to help with the preparations." Luna nods sleepily. Violina presses the violin into her hand and pushes it into the boat. Then she quickly directs it across the river to her clothes. "Here, it's still a bit damp from the morning dew, but you can put it on," says Violina and hands her dress to Luna. Luna's eyes are still half-closed. "Well, you might be a sleeping cap for me," Violina murmurs and helps Luna put on the dress. Then she continues to steer the boat to the fairground. You are lucky. The festival has not started yet, and the preparations are in full swing. All elves have something to do and run around excitedly.

Long tables with white ceilings stand around the large stage. Some elves bring shiny crystal glasses to the tables; others distribute silver cutlery. Elves with high white chef hats place huge pies with strawberries and cherries on the charts. And the smallest elves scurry around in between and scatter colorful flowers. Next to the stage is the elven Queen's throne, which already adorned with flowers. "Oh, that's nice!" Violina whispers. "Come on, Luna, let's practice again quickly," she says, reaching for her violin. "One, two, three, go! "But what is it? You only hear a croak. Luna has opened her mouth wide, but not a single sound comes out. She tries so hard that her head turns completely red. Violina also tries to elicit some beautiful sounds from her violin.

But there is only a loud squeak. "What will it be? Is that your surprise?" Giggles, a dark voice Elf Teacher Jackal stands behind them and laughs. "Oh, Mr. Jackal, you have to help us,"

Violina says desperately. "We slept outside tonight, and my violin got soaked from the rope! And I think Luna got a cold; she can't sing a sound!" Thick elven tears are already rolling down Violin's cheeks.

Mr. Jackal comfortably puts his arm around her shoulders. "Oh, we'll have it right away," he says reassuringly. "You can borrow my violin; I'll get it from home. And Luna first drinks hot tea. Violina nods and fetches tea for Luna. The elves sit sadly on a sheet, waiting for teacher jackal and drinking tea." Can you already say something? ", Violina asks after every sip Luna takes. But Luna shakes her head again and again. Finally, Mr. Jackal comes back. He hands Violina his violin." Here, practice a little more so that you can take care of yourself she's used to, "he says with a smile. Violina carefully strokes the bow over the strings. Soon it sounds perfect." It's a shame that you can't lend your voice to Luna, "says Violina sadly." Yes, that would be good" says Luna. Mr. Jackal grins. "Why are you laughing?" Asks Luna. "It's not funny!"

Mr. Jackal grins even more. "The voice is already back!" "Right," says Luna, "I said something!" Now she has to laugh too. "Well, now quickly to your seats," murmurs Mr. Jackal. "The elf queen has just come; the festival is starting!" they have not even noticed that all the other elves are already sitting at the tables. The elf queen is now majestically walking to her throne.

Luna and Violina dash to the stage. They excitedly wait behind the curtain until it's their turn. The ceremonial elf is saying: "Dear Queen, we are delighted that you are celebrating your one hundred and twenty-seventh birthday with us. All fairies congratulate you from the bottom of their heart and wish you a wonderful celebration. And at the beginning of our anniversary, two little elves want to recite the poem for you. Raise the curtain for Luna and Violina!"

The two elves step forward solemnly. Then they play and sing their little melody. It sounds beautiful and magical. The whole Elf people cheer, and even the Queen says this is the most beautiful song she has ever heard. The little elves shine. They hug and thankfully wave to Mr. Jackal. They have never been so happy in their lives!

Chapter 7:
Where's Mom Duck

At a large pond in the middle of the green, Mama Duck is standing in her nest and is very proud when the offspring hatch from the eggs. The little ducks break the shells and stick out their little heads. Then they wiggle their butts and shake the rest of the bowl off their bottom. Mama Duck nudges each of them lovingly with her beak. The little ones immediately know that this is the mom. Then the mom jumps into the water and one after the other jumps after. They swim in a line across the pond—the proud mom away from the front. But, oh dear, what is that? A chick has not yet hatched. It rumbles back and forth and rolls back and forth in the nest. With a lot of momentum, it tumbles onto the meadow, and the egg breaks on a stone.

The eggshell flies around, and the little duck shakes a lot. It looks around carefully. Well, there is nobody there. Hmm, weird. So, the duckling waddles off to find his mom. After a short time, the duckling meets a frog. The frog sits on a branch by the water and croaks. "Hooray!" Thinks the duckling. "It has to be a mom." It runs to the frog and happily croaks with it. The frog looks at the duck: "What are you doing here?" Asks the frog. The duckling replies: "I croak with you, mom!" The frog shakes his head: "I'm not your mom!" He says and hops away.

The duckling is sad, he thought it found Its mom. It continues to waddle with its head hanging. After a few steps, it encounters a bird. The bird is chirping happily. The duckling looks at the bird and thinks: "This is not croaking, but it has feathers.

Maybe that's my mom." And then it sits down next to the bird and croaks loudly. The bird is outraged: "Why are you covering my beautiful singing with your quack?" He asks. Then he pecks the duckling on the head and flies away. Now the duckling is sad, and tears roll down his cheeks. "I will never find my mom again!" She sobs softly to herself. A fox comes to the duckling. "Well, duckling, why are you so sad?" Asks the fox. "I'm looking for my mom. I'm all alone!" Says the duckling. The fox grins sneakily and says: "Come with me. Together we will find your mom. "The duckling is happy: "Hooray!" and runs after the fox. After a while, the duckling asks the fox: "How long are we going to run? We're almost in the forest. "The fox answers:" Don't worry. Your mom is there and waiting for you. "

The fox has no intention of finding the mom. He wants to lure the duckling into the forest to eat it under the protection of the trees. The fox grins and thinks: "It's too easy. I don't even have to wear the duckling; it runs into the forest on its own. "Once at the edge of the forest, the duckling stops: "But it is dark there in the forest!" It says fearfully. "You don't have to be afraid!" Says the fox. "I hid your mom there, so she's safe. "Sure, what from?" Asks the duckling. The fox answers in a worried voice:

"You know, there are many angry animals that would love to eat you. But don't be afraid, I'm not one of them! "Just as they wanted to continue, a bear stands in the way: "Well, fox? Where do you want to go with the duckling?"

He asks. The fox ducks in terror: "Hello, big bear, where are you from so suddenly? I only help the duckling to find his mom!" The bear looks at the duckling. Then he asks in a growl, "Is the little duckling, right?" The duckling jumps up and down: "Yes! The fox hid them in the forest because there are so many angry animals. "The bear immediately suspects what the fox is up to." "So, there are a lot of bad animals here," he grumbles. Then he looks at the fox suspiciously: "Well, luckily you are not one of them, fox. Right? "The fox shakes his head quickly:" No, no, but of course not. I just wanted to help poor duckling. "The bear takes the duckling protectively in his paws and says:" Well, that's great that the fox helped you here. Now, I'm going to make it better.

Your mom is no longer in the forest. I think she went to the pond to look for you. She misses you very much, you know? "Then he looks at the fox again and asks with a threatening look:" Is it true, fox? "The fox nods his head very quickly:" Yes, now that you say it falls it me again. She ran to the pond earlier. "Then the fox looks at the duckling:" Your mom is back at the lake. I had completely forgotten that, yes, yes. "So, the bear takes the duckling with it. The two meet the bird on the way to the pond. The duckling trembles. "What have you got?" Asks the bear. The duckling ducks and whispers: "The bird pecked me because I thought it was my mom." The bear looks at the bird angrily and grumbles: "I look into your face here; the duckling probably speaks the truth.

You also must help, but you didn't help poor duckling!" Then he takes a deep breath: "We'll talk about that when I come back," he says, and carries the duckling on. The bird flutters away quickly. Next, the two meet the frog. The bear looks at the duckling: "Did the frog hurt you too?" The duckling replies: "No, he just jumped away." The bear looks at the frog angrily and grumbles: "I look at your face here; the duckling probably speaks the truth. You also must help, but you didn't help poor duckling!" Then he takes a deep breath: "We'll talk about that when I come back," he says, and carries the duckling on. The frog hops away quickly. When the two arrive at the pond, the duckling is very happy when it sees the mom.

It cheers and jumps headlong into the lake: "Thank you, dear bear! Calls it to the bear. "And please also thank the fox of mine." The bear grumbles back loudly: "Little ducks are welcome. And don't worry, I will indeed thank the fox powerfully from you. "When the fox hears this, he picks up his ears, startled. "Oh dear, now I'm still on the collar." He thinks and runs as fast as he can over all mountains. The fox has never been seen since. The bear still keeps a watchful eye on the little duckling, so that a clever fox never gets stupid thoughts again.

Chapter 8:
A Snowman Saves Christmas

O nce upon a time, there was a snowman who lived in the Christmas wonderland. But it wasn't a treehouse. It was a real house in a tree. It was normal in the Christmas wonderland, and there were also gingerbread houses, huge Christmas trees and a lot more fantastic. But let's get back to our snowman, whose greatest wish was to be a Christmas elf. However, only elves could become Christmas elves. So, it was written in the big Christmas book. Still, the snowman tried year after year. The boy even disguised himself once as an elf to get to the great Christmas factory. But he noticed the Nachleben at the gate. Maybe his carrot had betrayed him on the face? Or perhaps he was just more spherical than everyone else. It would work this year because the snowman had a great idea.

The boy wanted to pack gifts himself and distribute them to the children. Could Santa not be angry with him for that? And he could finally put the smile so longed for on the children's faces. The first thing was to get the presents. But where to get from and not steal? He had to make money somehow. But what should he do? He was incredibly good at sledding. But you couldn't make money from it. Then he thought of something. He slipped happily and began to form little snowballs. Then he took a sign and sat in the snow. The sign read: "Every ball three thalers." That should work. Everyone likes snowball fights, but the snowman sat in a vain hour after hour. Nobody even bought a snowball. So, he asked the blacksmith if he could help. But he only laughed out loud.

"What do you want to help me?" Asked the smith. "If you stand by the fire with me, you will melt. Do you want to serve me as drinking water?" "That's right." Thought the snowman, it had to be something where it was cold. So, he went to the ice cream factory. Large ice blocks made there to build igloos. But here too, the snowman was laughed at. "How do you want to help me?" Asked the factory manager. "The blocks are so heavy if you want to push them, your thin stick arms break." "That's right." Thought the snowman again, it has to be something where it is cold, and the work is not too difficult. So, the snowman went to the ice-cream seller. He was taken with the idea and said: "You are a good ice cream seller! You are never too cold, and if ice is missing for cooling, we simply take something from you. "

When the snowman heard this, he was startled. "Ice cream from me?" He asked. "I think I was wrong in the door," he said, running away quickly. The snowman was sad now. Nothing boy tried worked. The boy sank to the ground in the middle of the city; His hat slipped over his sad button eyes. He took his violin and played a Christmas carol. It had always helped him when he was sorry. When he was playing, he was so thoughtful that he didn't even notice the people passing him throwing some change. It was when a stranger given by said: "A wonderful Christmas carol. It is one of my favorites. Keep playing snowman," he listened. He pushed his hat up and saw the change in front of him. "That's money!" He said softly and kept playing. "That's money!"

He cried out and continued playing. He grinned all over his face and sang with all his heart's content: "Tomorrow there will be something for children. Tomorrow we will be happy. "With the newly earned money, he bought gifts and wrapping paper on a doll there and a car here. It was packed and laced diligently and passed the cord through the hole. "One on the right, one on the left—yes, the snowman comes and brings it!" But wait. How are the gifts supposed to get to the children from here? The snowman considered. "I can't wear it. But I don't have a Christmas sleigh either. And Santa Claus will hardly lend me his. The reindeer would also want to eat my carrot." The snowman was incredibly good at sledding on a sled, but it wasn't always just downhill. So, what to do? The snowman also had a great idea here. He tied the presents onto a snail. Snails can carry a lot. That would work. Just when he does, a Christmas elf came by.

"What will it be when it's done?" Asked the Christmas elf. The snowman proudly stood next to his snail. "This is my Christmas snail! And I'm handing out gifts to the kids this year." The Christmas elf looked at the snowman and the snail in amazement. "I'd laugh now if it weren't so sad," he said then. "You already know that a snail is too slow to deliver gifts to all the children in the world? I mean, it would be too lazy to supply this village itself. "The joyful grin faded from the snowman, and the elf continued: "Unfortunately, these are also far too few gifts. You would need a million billion times more but it doesn't matter anyway. Christmas is canceled anyway! "When the snowman heard that, he no longer understood the world." Christmas is canceled? The Christmas elf nodded: "And whether that works. Santa Claus got sick and can't give gifts."

"Nazanin" breathed the snowman in astonishment and looked at the elf incredulously. "Santa Claus can't get sick at all." The Christmas elf nodded again: "That's right. Usually not but this year it is so cold that even Christmas elves are too cold for it. "The snowman became nervous:" But Christmas, so Christmas... so, what about Christmas? "He ran around in a hectic circle and spoke to himself:" No, no, no, no, that cannot be. A Christmas without gifts is not a Christmas. "The Christmas elf interrupted the snowman." Christmas is Christmas without gifts. The gifts have always been more and almost too much over the past few years. "The snowman slumped briefly and breathed out." Then he stood up straight and said:" But with gifts, it is a lot more beautiful."

The Christmas elf shook his head: "Christmas is the festival of charity. There is no need for presents. "The snowman spun around and said softly:" Yes, that's right. "Then he took one of his presents and held it up to the Christmas elf:" But look how beautiful the presents are. With a gift like that, I can show my love for my neighbor much better than without. "Then he made the gift disappear behind his back and looked sadly at the Christmas elf." Look, it's gone now. Isn't that sad? Imagine the many little sad googly eyes standing in front of a Christmas tree under which there are no gifts. Now tell the children that we don't need gifts because Christmas is the festival of charity! "The Christmas elf gave in: "Ok, maybe you're right. But what should we do?

It's too cold!" The snowman tossed the gift aside and slid to the Christmas elf: "Ha! Exactly! It's too cold! For Santa Claus. But I'm a snowman!" Then he turned in a circle and began to sing: "I'm never too cold, I will grow old. I can hurry and hurry, hand out gifts to the children. You just have to help me with stuff and team. Take me to Santa Claus quickly. "The Christmas elf covered his ears: "Now just stop singing. I'll take you there. "The snowman jumped in the air with joy:" Yeah! Hey, it almost rhymed. You could also sing a song." Snowman talked for a while on the way to Santa Claus—to the regret of the Christmas elf. Arrived at Santa Claus, he was shocked to see a snowman at home. Usually, there were only Christmas elves there. But Santa Claus loved the idea that Christmas shouldn't cancel.

Because he also thought that Christmas with gifts merely is more beautiful. But how should the snowman distribute so many presents? The snowman chewed nervously on his lips. He was so close to living his most prominent dream. "We don't have to distribute all the presents," he said then. "Everyone gets a little less this year. It's still better than nothing, isn't it? "Santa looked at the snowman:" I don't think the idea is terrible. That should work! But what do you want to drive the gifts with? You can't have my sled!" The snowman was on the verge of despair. "Just solve this one problem, and my dream will come true," the boy thought to himself. Then he said sheepishly: "So, I'm a pretty good sled!" Then the Christmas elf interfered: "Oh, that's all nonsense!

Then you only deliver to the children who live at the bottom of a mountain? Or how should I imagine that? "But Santa Claus raised his hand and moved his fingers as if he were scratching the air. A massive snow slide appeared from nowhere under the snowman. Then Santa said: "You're such a good sled tobogganer. This snow mountain will accompany you. It is a never-ending snow slope. So, you can sled anywhere quickly. "The snowman looked at the vast snow mountain and said: "That Is "then he suddenly jumped in the air and shouted: "yes, the hammer! Tobogganing forever! That's not how I imagined it in my wildest dreams. "

The snowman was happy, like never before. But Santa Claus raised his index finger again and said warningly: "But watch out for the fireplaces! I've already burned my bottom!" But the snowman was cold: "Oh, I have so much snow with me, if I burn my bottom, I'll just make myself a new one—ha-ha." Then he grinned at Santa, jumped on his sled and he was gone. The snowman saved Christmas, that was too cold, but just right for the snowman!

Chapter 9:
The Oldest Unicorn

On the tallest hill in the magical land lived the oldest of all the unicorns. Nobody ever came to visit him, and he had lived so long that most had forgotten he was even up there. His only friend was the witch, but even she was too busy to visit him.

One day Spring woke up and found there was something wrong with her horn. It didn't want to glow, and it wouldn't sparkle. Its color was dim, and she couldn't feel any magic in it. Spring quickly visited all her friends but none of them knew what to do.

"I'm sorry, I'm not sure why this is happening," Fay told her.

"It's never happened to me," Cosmic said.

"Perhaps it was something you ate last night," Crystal suggested.

"I hope it's not contagious," Spring said.

"You should go see the witch and ask her," Odd told her.

Spring did what he said, and she went to go see the witch. She was so sad without her magical horn. A unicorn can't just have a normal horn. Every unicorn needs to have a magical horn that glows brightly, and glitters and sparkles.

When Spring got to the witch's garden, she was sure that the witch would be able to help using her magic.

"I'm sorry Spring, but I'm not sure why your horn isn't working," the witch told her. "I don't think I've ever seen this happen before, but I think I know someone who has."

"Who?" Spring asked with a slight smile.

"The oldest unicorn," the witch answered. "He lives up on the tallest hill in the magical land. He is so old that he has probably seen something like this happen before. You should go visit and ask him. Remember to bring him a gift when you do."

Spring thanked the witch and started her long journey to the tallest hill in the magical land. She didn't even know that someone lived up there until now. She was hoping that the oldest unicorn would be kind and help her.

On the way she stopped to pick some flowers and fruit as a gift for the oldest unicorn. It was hard to carry them all because she couldn't use her magic horn. She met some fairies along the way and asked them kindly to make her a basket out of wood and string. They did this for her, and she was able to carry the flowers and fruits up the hill in the basket.

It was the middle of the day when she finally reached the top of the hill. She was surprised by what she saw. There was a small, but lovely house right at the top. There was a garden filled with flowers and a big tree that dropped fruit to the floor.

Spring walked up to the house and knocked on the front door. She put the basket down and waited for the oldest unicorn to answer.

"Go away!" she heard the oldest unicorn yell from inside the house.

Spring was shocked at first, but she knocked again and said, "Oldest unicorn, I need your help."

"I don't care, go away."

"But I brought you a gift."

It was silent for a moment then the oldest unicorn opened the door and looked down at the basket of fruit and flowers. He looked up at Spring.

"What do you want?" He asked.

"I need your help; my horn isn't magical anymore and no one knows what's wrong with it."

"What makes you think I can help?"

"You're the oldest unicorn and the witch said you might have seen this happen before. Can you please help me?"

The oldest unicorn frowned, then sighed and said, "Okay, I will help you, but you have to do exactly as I say."

"Oh, I will!"

For the rest of the day Spring did everything the old unicorn asked her to. She tended to his garden for him, picked the fruit off the ground, and cleaned his house for him. Spring wasn't sure why she was doing all this, but she hoped it would help fix her horn. It was getting late and Spring had done all that the oldest unicorn had asked, but her horn still didn't have any magic.

"What's the big idea?" Spring asked. "I've done all the chores you asked me to, and my horn isn't fixed yet."

"You're not done, there is still more you need to do."

"I think you're wrong. I think you just wanted to get me to do all the chores you were too lazy to do and you weren't going to help me at all."

The oldest unicorn gasped and frowned at Spring, "How dare you? Do you think I would just help you for free? You must first do things for me and then I will reward you."

"But I brought you a gift!"

"It is good manners to bring someone a gift when visiting their home, especially if they are your elder. That does not mean I will help you. First you do something for me and then I help you. Now go over there and eat the fruit that falls from the tree. That will fix your horn."

Spring was angry but she did as he said. She ate the fruit and it worked. She felt all the magic come back to her horn and it started to glow once again. She jumped for joy and cheered, but then she spotted the oldest unicorn, still angry with her.

She bowed her head to him and said, "I'm sorry, oldest unicorn. You were right and I should have respected you more."

"It's alright," he said. "You are young, and too impulsive. You still need to learn how to slow down and wait for things that life will bring you. Just remember from now on to always respect your elders and use good manners. If you can respect others, then they will respect you too. Now go home quick before it gets too dark. If you or any of your friends ever have a problem with your horn, you know where to find me. Remember to bring a gift."

Spring said goodbye and ran home to show her friends her new magical horn.

Chapter 10:
Brindle is Scared

Brindle was a beautiful and magical unicorn. Before she went to bed each night, she would brush her long silky mane a thousand times. Her mother would help her, and it was Brindle's favorite time of the day. She would talk about her day, and her mother would listen.

"I played soccer today," said Brindle.

"Did you score any goals?" asked her mother.

"I scored one, but that was all." Brindle polished her golden horn until it was extra-shiny.

"Well, did you try your hardest?" asked her mother.

"I always try my hardest," said Brindle with pride.

"Then that is all that matters," said her mother. "If you try your hardest, then you can do nothing more."

"Can I tell you all about my adventures in the glade?" asked Brindle.

"How about in the morning?" asked her mother. "Look at how late it is? The sun went down a long time ago, and the moon is high in the sky."

SHORT BEDTIME TALES FOR KIDS

"I am tired," said a sleepy Brindle.

Brindle finished polishing her golden horn, and she got into her bed. Her mother read her a bedtime story and tucked her in, giving Brindle a kiss on the head. The light was turned off, but the room still had a glow in it, partly from the small nightlight, and partly from the moon.

It had been a long, fun day for Brindle, and she was excited to rest and dream. She had almost fallen asleep when a noise woke her.

"Hello," said Brindle.

The room was silent. Brindle looked around, but the room was exactly how it had been when she had fallen asleep. She lay there for a moment, scanning the room. It was full of shadows, and that made Brindle a little afraid.

"Mom!" shouted Brindle.

There was soon a clip-clopping noise as her mother came up the stairs and into her room.

"What is the matter?" asked her mother.

"I thought that I heard a noise," said Brindle.

"Hmm," said her mother. "It must have been the wind. Noises sound different at night, but they are no different from the noises that come during the day."

79 | P a g .

"I think that it is gone now," said Brindle. "I should go back to sleep."

"Goodnight," said her mother.

Brindle soon fell asleep, but, again, she was woken.

She was sure that she had heard a noise, and this time, it had come from the closet. She lay in bed and stared at the closet, convinced that something was in there. Perhaps it was a goblin.

Brindle did not like feeling afraid. She wished that she could be brave and have no fear.

"Mom!" shouted Brindle again.

There was a clip-clopping sound again, and soon her mother was in the room. This made her feel less afraid.

"I felt scared," said Brindle. "I thought that there might be a goblin in the closet, but that's stupid. I wish that I were not so afraid."

"You cannot help being afraid," said her mother.

"But I want to be brave," said Brindle.

"Being scared does not mean that you are not brave," said her mother.

"It doesn't?"

"Of course not. Being brave is about accepting your fear. I have been scared and afraid many times," said her mother with a smile.

"You have?" Brindle was excited to hear more.

"I was afraid when you went out by yourself for the first time. I was afraid when I moved here to start a new life. I was afraid when I had to walk home in the dark one time. But I was brave because I accepted my fear and did not let it control me," said her mother.

"How do I accept my fear?" asked Brindle.

"Well, that takes practice. You have to let your fear be your friend. It has to live inside of you, and then you have to do things anyway. That is how you become brave and courageous. That is how you face your fears."

"Face my fears?" Brindle did not like the sound of that.

"If you can make friends with your fear, you will see that you can control it. Look at the closet over there. You think that there might be a goblin inside. That is the fear inside trying to control you. Come on, let's face it together," said her mother.

Brindle was still scared, but she felt braver with her mother beside her. The two unicorns walked over to the closet, and Brindle opened the door.

It was empty.

"Where else do you want to look?" asked her mother.

"How about under the bed?" Brindle was feeling a little braver now.

"Let's go and take a look," said her mother.

The two unicorns clopped over to the bed and looked under. It was a little scary and dark, but there was no goblin under there.

"I feel a little silly now," said Brindle. "There was nothing there all along."

"That does not make you silly, Brindle. It only shows that your fear is inside of you and not in your outside world. If your fear is inside of you, you can accept it and control it. That is what bravery is all about, and you have been a very brave unicorn tonight," said her mother.

"I have?" Brindle was prouder than she had ever been.

"I think that you are brave enough to sleep," said her mother. "Now that you have made friends with your fear, you are in control."

"Thank you, Mother," said Brindle. "Goodnight."

"Goodnight," said her mother as she turned off the light.

Brindle was still a little scared, but the fear was her friend now.
She soon fell asleep and had wonderful dreams of meadows and
rainbows.

Chapter 11:
Honesty is the Key

I n one of the old villages there was a unicorn called Jack who lived with his mother in a small house after the death of his father, who passed away when Jack was young with a small horn due to his severe illness.

Jack's mother used to take care of her son very seriously, and this care was not limited to caring for food, drink and clothing, but his mother was interested in teaching her child the good morals, such as sincerity and to be kind to those he meets in his life, and that these morals can help him to contribute in his community leaving a good impact in the hearts of all people.

His will is to be a perfect unicorn, and possesses all their beautiful attributes, because they are known for their attractive and valued personalities.

They are an example of goodness, kindness and love. His mother wanted Jack to be the symbol of these qualities among his townspeople, and she made a great effort towards that.

Jack had an uncle working in trade between unicorn countries, Jack went with him on some commercial trips in order to be able to bear responsibility, as these trips needed patience and seriousness, in which the traveler travelled long distances.

They reached remote cities in order to be supplied with goods and resell them for the unicorn in the village where Jack and his mother lived, and in the villages next to it.

Jack was learning from his uncle the concepts of selling and trading, and how to be an expert in the process of buying and selling through clarity with others and not deceiving them, and his main rule was to avoid lying, Jack learned these principles well from his uncle before being allowed to travel with him.

During this trip, Jack dealt with a short but very important story. While he was with the caravan on their way to trade, a group of thieving wolves attacked them, surrounded the convoy including with the ones in it, seized the goods they carried, and took their food and money.

When one of the wolves arrived at Jack, the wolf asked him in a threatening tone: You little boy, how many golden coins do you carry? All of this is now ours.

He answered steadfastly: I carry thirty pieces of gold

Here, this wolf drowned in a wave of laughter, and ridiculed Jack's answer to him saying: You are very funny, boy, you are too young to bear this amount, do not pretend that you are rich, this is funny.

Then another wolf came from the gang members who cut off the road and asked him the same question. He answered the same answer, and the other wolf mocked him, saying: Our leader must see this himself and laugh, come with me.

They took him to the leader of the gang. When Jack reached the leader, he quietly asked him: Tell me how much coins you have, and do not cheat, because I will know right away.

He replied: I am not bluffing, I really told them that I had thirty pieces of gold

So, he asked him: Why do you stick to this excessive honesty and not evade the correct answer, as did the other unicorns in the convoy with this gang to preserve their money?

So, Jack brought out the thirty pieces he owned and told the gang leader: I promised my mother that I would not lie, and I would not betray my mother and my promise to her no matter what might cause me to hide the truth.

Here the gang leader was surprised, and he remembered that in his robbery of this convoy, he had betrayed his father's past command not to follow the path of evil.

At that point, the gang leader did not take control of himself and wept, affected by what Jack said to him, and told Jack: You did not betray your mother's promise and I will not betray my father's promise as well.

The gang leader ordered the release of all members of the convoy and returned to them all what were taken from them, and worked to serve and guard the commercial convoy until they reached the city they intended.

He thanked Jack in particular saying: I really thank you for this honesty and courage that awoke the goodness and extinguished the evil inside me, if you need him at any time I will help you.

Jack bid farewell to the former gang leader and left in peace with his family.

This gang stopped cutting people off and taking their money by force due to Jack's honesty, telling the truth, and keeping his promise to his mother.

Jack found his uncle coming to him with pride, he hugged him happily before his mother came to do the same, everyone was proud of him and the news spread among his town and friends.

He became an example of honesty and trust, and many merchants asked Jack to work with them for their confidence in his morals.

They also showed their great admiration for his mother and for the ideal education methods that she applied, and they praised her for bearing hardships and looking after her son alone after the death of her husband.

Chapter 12:
Mary and the Unicorn

A long time ago, there was a little girl named Mary. She was the only daughter in a rich family with a strong reputation in her country.

Her father was one of the richest, wisest and most intelligent men in the city. As for her mother, she was a big fan of fairy tales, she owned a very huge library full of fairy tales and ancient legendary stories, she was also writing some of them and reading them to her daughter Mary, who unfortunately did not like these stories and never believed in them.

One day Mary was sad and sitting alone in her room, she was always missing the magic touch in her life, she needed some surprise and imagination, but she did not allow anyone to help her, she kept her mother and friends away from her most of the time.

Her mother came that day to her room and said: Mary, my dear, do you want me to tell a story? I will not read stories that you did not like before, I will read a new and funny one.

Mary looked at her mother sadly and said with an unhappy voice: No, I do not want to hear anything.

The mother was a little disappointed that her daughter refused her help, she went to her library to return the story back to its place and then went to sleep wishing that she would wake up to find Mary in a better condition.

After the mother left the library, that story that she was going to read to her daughter fell to the ground, she had not put it on the shelf properly.

While the poor mother was asleep, Mary felt in her room a bit of regret, she felt that she was rude and impatient with her mother while all what she was trying to do is helping her.

Mary knew that her mother was in pain when she saw her only daughter isolated, lonely and sad, but Mary did not know what to do, she did not like those stories of unicorns, Santa Claus or other fairy tales.

Mary always said to herself and her mother: I do not know why you believe the existence of these beings, what is the use of loving something that does not even exist, you are all liars and I do not like talking to you.

And when one of her friends said to her: Mary, the unicorns are real, we all know that even if we do not see them.

Mary replied to her: Of course not, I have never seen a unicorn before, not even in my dreams, as long as I have not seen one of them, they do not exist for me.

Then she turned her face and went away to go home and stopped playing with them.

Suddenly Mary decided to give an opportunity that might change her mind, perhaps her mother knows more than her, and maybe she has already seen a unicorn before, but she cannot reveal it.

She rose from her bed and left the room with courageous steps; she quietly closed the door so that her mother would not wake up as she was sleeping in the room next to her.

She thought about going back and sticking to her thoughts, but she was very sad when she saw her mother's face and her disappointed expressions, she continued walking until she entered the library.

Mary was confused; she did not know what to read from this huge number of stories.

She thought, I can read about Cinderella.

She looked a little about her stories and then said: No, I want something more interesting. My mom has read this story to me many times before, so I think I saved it.

On her way, she found books for Santa Claus as well, but she said: We are still in the middle of the year, I will try to read it before Christmas.

Then she found a book on the ground, it's the book that her mother wanted to read to her, she took it and looked at it and said: A unicorn story, maybe this is what I'm searching for, I have always loved these creatures but I have hidden these feelings because I have not seen them before, I have decided, I will read it and give it chance.

She took the book with her and went back to the room, she liked the unicorn drawings so much, and she loved their wings and colorful horns as she liked their cheerful and courageous characters.

She read the story in amazement and great admiration, she even read it three times in a row, but she was not completely happy yet; she said to herself: I loved them very much, but I still cannot see them and this makes me very upset whenever I hear about them. If only I could see one of them, I would go and read all the books in the library, but my feeling that they are not real prevents me from that.

She put the book on her table heavily and sat next to the window watching trees and birds until she slept in peace, and suddenly she heard knockings on the window, Mary woke up to find what made her heart dance from the intensity of joy, it was a unicorn! He was flying his wings in front of the window while smiling at her.

Mary opened the window happily and said to him: You are real! I am very happy, but I want to apologize as well because I doubted you, I really needed to see you.

Unicorn said to her: No need to apologize, my dear, but even if you cannot see things, this does not mean that they are not real. For example, you cannot see the love that your mother and father hold for you, but it certainly exists and you certainly believe in it, I do not have to live with you at home to be real, I live in your imagination and in your little mind, you can talk to me at any time and make sure that I hear you and if you want to tell me something write it on a paper and put it in front of your window and I will read it.

Mary said in astonishment: You are very kind, I promise to become like you and show my love for my mother and father, and even my friends, I will go to play with them when I have the opportunity

The unicorn said to her: I knew you were a kind and beautiful girl, you have a lot of love inside your heart, so go now and spread it to the world.

The unicorn turned around to leave after changing this girl's life, possibly forever.

The mother woke up to find her daughter busy in one of the drawings. Mary was holding her pen and drawing with it on a paper on her desk while she was charmingly smiling.

When Mary saw her mother, she took the paper and presented it to her, it was a drawing of the unicorn who visited her. The mother was very happy of her daughter and sat next to her while she was completing the drawing.

Mary hugged her mother and said to her: My mother, I love you.

Mary's mother was so happy and said: Me too, my dear, me too.

Chapter 13:

White Sands, Blue Water and Dragons

Tommy Robinson was born and raised on the beautiful Caribbean Ocean. He was only a young boy when his Dad took him fishing out on the clear blue ocean. The family lived in Palmas Bellas, Panama, and Tommy was just 9 years old. Tommy's Dad was a priest, and the family had lived in the country of Panama for centuries. The Robinson lineage was heralded as one of honor and nobility. Tommy was psychic, and his Dad did not like it!

Tommy had learned about his gifts when he was a toddler and had been able to move things around in his bedroom from his crib. At first, he was afraid to tell anyone because even he was scared by his own abilities. He just knew it was not normal. One night, Tommy's Dad walked in while he was levitating his Teddy Bear, which was in his toy box and trying to bring it to him in his crib. The door opened, and there was the Teddy, floating in the air and Tommy standing up in his crib, holding the top rail with a look on his face that his Father had never seen before. The Teddy dropped to the floor suddenly, and Tommy started to cry. He always remembered that his Dad didn't say anything to him about it then or any time after, but he knew his Dad was not happy about his only son being what he thought of as a freak.

On the day of the fishing outing, Tommy asked his Dad about the Caribbean Sea, and if there were any strange creatures living in it. Of course, his Dad did not like this question and was not interested in the subject. Since it was to be a fishing trip, Tommy's Dad wanted to get him interested in the sport and had bought a rod and reel for both of them and some fishing gear for the outing. The big fishing boat rocked and rolled in the waves when they reached the open ocean.

Tommy liked the feeling; his Dad hated it and got seasick. Eventually, the captain called out that they were coming up on the fishing spot, and the boat began to slow down, and finally, the motors could be heard powering down. The huge anchor splashed down into the ocean, and everyone started fiddling with their fishing gear.

Everyone found a spot and set up some deck chairs with their snacks and coffee thermoses nearby. Tommy and his Dad did the same, but Tommy wanted to stand. He kept peering down over the side of the boat into the dark and foreboding looking water. "Hey, Dad, you can't see down into the water," Tommy exclaimed. His Dad didn't answer as he was busy trying to put the live bait on his hook. Tommy said, "here, let me help you, Pop." And Mr. Robinson stopped what he was doing and froze for the moment while he considered his son's offer. "Okay, boy, you show me you can do it better than I can then," he said, handing Tommy the rod and the bait can. Tommy grabbed up one of the squirming worms, and to his Dad's surprise, the thing went completely still, as though it was actually helping Tommy to hook itself. "How did you do that so easily?" his Dad asked with a very puzzled look on his face. "I dunno," Tommy answered.

Tommy handed the rod back to his Dad and baited his own rod, and they both cast out their lines. Somebody, a few people down the row, got a big bite. Everyone turned their attention to the man as he reeled in a large fish that looked like it should be good eating. That got everyone excited, and soon, just about all of them had caught something. Some caught more big fish, and some caught sharks and other fish that had to be cut loose.

Then Tommy felt a tug on his line. It was strong, and little Tommy stood up and grabbed his pole with both hands. His Dad watched him with admiration and thought to himself that he had never seen his son take charge like this. New territory for sure. When Tommy got the catch pulled almost up to the surface, it really started to fight. He fought back and eventually stepped back as he reeled and reeled, giving the catch no slack at all. His father was amazed. It looked to him as though Tommy had done this many times, but he knew for a fact that this was Tommy's first-time fishing.

Then, as everyone watched, Tommy snagged the catch up out of the water and flipped it into the boat. The only sound that could be heard was that of the waves lapping up against the side of the boat. Nobody could believe their eyes in what they saw. It looked like it had legs instead of fins, and it had a head like a tiny horse. The thing whipped its head around, pulled out the hook, which oddly was attached to its tail and ran down the deck and bounded up onto the railing just like a little monkey would have. It sat upon the railing for a good minute or so and turned around to look back at all the gawking fishermen. Everyone knew what it looked like, but still, nobody spoke. Then Tommy did!

"It's a baby dragon," he said to much noise and disagreement on the part of some of the other fishermen. "It is," he said again and began to walk slowly towards the little thing. "Don't be afraid," he said, and then in his mind, he heard distinct words and had to assume they came from the little creature. "Why would I be afraid of the likes of you lot?" were the words he heard. He remembered his gifts and stilled his mind. Tommy had been practicing something called mindfulness, and it was easy for him to clear his mind so he could answer the little beast. "Are you a dragon?" Tommy mentally asked the creature. "Well, what else would I be? I'd like to know now, wouldn't I," the beast answered. A moment, and then Tommy thought back to answer again, "my name is Tommy, what is your name?" he asked.

"I am Drake!" the baby dragon replied. "So, you are a dragon, then?" Tommy asked once more. "Are you blind? Of course, I am, I thought we already had that established." Said the young dragon. By this time, some of the other fishermen were becoming antsy, and Tommy could hear some shuffling around, and some of them talking with a low voice amongst themselves. Tommy's Dad, on the other hand, was speechless. He sensed that his son had something going on with the amazing little creature but didn't want to believe what he now found obvious. Watching his son staring at the Dragon and the baby staring right back at him told him there could only be one possible answer. They were communicating.

"I have many questions," Tommy mentally asked the dragon. "Then why don't you ask them instead of staring at me like a moron," the baby said. "You're a cheeky little dragon, aren't you?" Tommy fired back. "Okay, this conversation is over," the dragon spat. "No, wait, I'm sorry then if I offended you. Look, it isn't every day that I get to talk to a dragon, so where can I find you so we can talk later?" Tommy asked. "If you are serious, I will meet you at noon tomorrow at Lighthouse Point, but you must come alone!" the baby said to Tommy. "I will be there," Tommy said, and with that, the little dragon plunged back into the depths and disappeared.

When Tommy turned around to face the crowd, every one of them stared at him speechlessly. His Dad just looked down at his feet and then took up his rod like nothing had happened and returned to his fishing activities. A few of the other fishermen grumbled and then followed suit.

Needless to say, the rest of the days outing was quiet at best, and Tommy wondered how they would all handle the fact that they had not only witnessed a psychic encounter, they had seen a real live dragon with their own eyes.

Tommy's Dad, being a man of the cloth, did not like it at all and wanted to speak to his son about it but somehow never did. Tommy was developing his powers, and nothing could stop it. He never questioned why he had them, but rather just used his mindfulness to access them in a productive manner. He no longer levitated things and kept pretty much to himself for the time being.

The next morning, Tommy arose and went down to eat breakfast with his family. It was summer vacation time, and school was out, so he had a lot of time on his hands. At the table, his Dad said grace as always, and then they ate. When they were done, Tommy's Dad said, "well, what are you up to today, son?" Tommy said, "I'm going to the beach to look for shells." His Father grunted his approval, and that was it for morning conversation.

Tommy finished his breakfast, and then went back up to his room to change into his swim trunks. Then, down the stairs and out the door he went, pulled out his bike, and started to peddle madly towards the beach. He hadn't realized it, but he was excited. Very excited, actually, and he wondered why the little dragon had become snagged in his line. Could it have been intentional? He let that thought dangle, as he reached the cove, and hid his bike in the rocks.

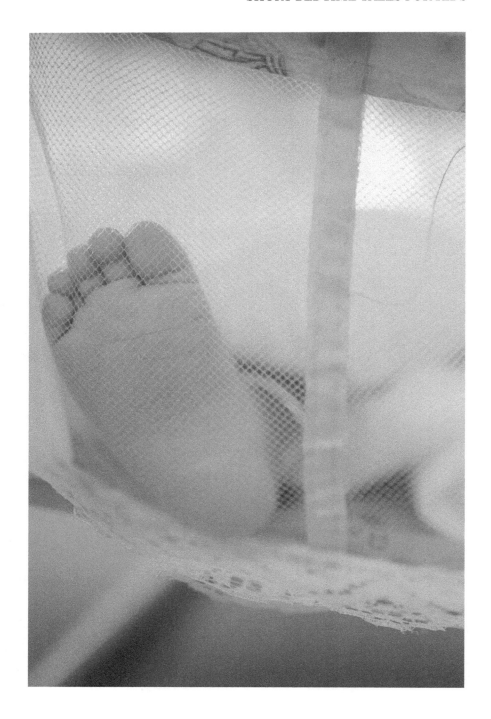

Chapter 14:
The Unicorn and
The Devilish Dragon

Brindle and her new monster friends wandered down and around and all about. Everyone was getting very tired and even though Zesty kept feeding them delicious things; they were starting to grow tired.

Skeleton kept out front, stopping continuously and looking around. He would nod and see that he had turned the wrong way and sometimes everyone had to backtrack.

This made everyone a little upset at times, but they had faith in their friend that he would get them all to the Dragon.

They rounded a curve, and then a corner, and then... there he was! Brindle had never seen a dragon before. This monster was huge!

He was also so beautiful. It looked like he was made of metal. So shiny, with the sun glinting off of all the armored scales. He was a very intimidating beast indeed. However, Brindle was over all her fear of monsters and was ready to help her new friend, Medusa... whatever it took.

Brindle approached, getting closer and closer. She realized her first impression of this monster being huge was greatly underestimated. It was gigantic. Brindle stopped for a moment.

"No, courage is best," Brindle said under her breath and went on. Closer and closer, and then...

"Stop right there, little unicorn," the beast had a very deep voice that matched his size. "What do you want?"

"Hi... my name is Brindle. My friends over there said you might be able to help our new friend," said Brindle, only a little afraid. "I know we just met. I want you to be honest when I ask for help. I will help you in return if you need. Or maybe I can owe you a favor. I don't know. We just need help?"

Brindle realized that that was not the best introduction she had ever done, but she was very nervous. She stopped rattling on and let the dragon speak. And he did.

"Hmm..." He said slowly. "It does depend on what kind of help you are asking for. You tell me what you want and then I will tell you whether I can help you or not."

"Fair enough," Brindle nodded. "My friend Medusa, over there... well... she has this thing she does that she does not want to do."

Brindle took a deep breath and said, "She looks at someone and then they turn to stone."

The old, metallic Dragon waited what felt like a lifetime to reply.

"Hmmm…" He said at last. "I have heard of this. Medusas are very rare. And they do turn anyone or anything they look at into stone. Including you and me, Brindle. This is a very dangerous friend you have. Are you sure you want to help her?"

"Oh yes I do!" said Brindle.

"Well, I may have a solution. Miss Medusa…"

"Yes?" asked Brindle's hooded friend.

"You have snakes on your head. How many snakes are there?" the Dragon asked.

"Ummm… Ten? Wait… one, two, three, four, five…" Medusa was counting her snakes. "Twelve… Yes… Twelve snakes."

"And your eyes, assuming they turn individuals to stone, makes thirteen sets of stone making eyes."

"I think I have a solution," Dragon nodded. "I will help you, Brindle. But when I am done, I will need you to do something for me. Are you prepared to exchange help for each other?"

Brindle thought for a moment. "Yes. We can do that. I adventure all the time. Another adventure would be a pleasure!"

"I like that attitude," said Dragon. "I need to forge some metal things for your new friend. So, everyone please stand back."

Brindle stepped back to her friends. Dragon saw they were at a safe distance and reached over to some metal rock and ripped a big chunk into its claws.

Then the Dragon began to bellow. Hotter and hotter his chest got. Finally, he coughed a bright flame into his hands where that metal was. Then Brindle saw the most amazing thing. Those huge clawed hands started to tinker and work with that hot metal. Brindle was amazed at how those big hands were making something so small!

Pounding and pounding. Working and working, that old Dragon forged and forged.

Finally, the Dragon breathed out some cold mist to cool down the metal.

"Done," the Dragon was all worked out. "Oh, by the way. I am the Devilish Dragon. Forge expert and maker of many things."

Brindle could have sworn that the Dragon was grinning.

Devilish Dragon took Medusa's hand and led her over to the new things he had created. Brindle and her friends were very curious but stayed back.

Dragon and Medusa talked and talked. Brindle watched Medusa pick up those little shiny things and stuff them under her hood.

Dragon and Medusa kept talking and Brindle overheard them trying to think about how they would know if it worked without trying it out.

It seemed that they were both very nervous about that.

Finally, Dragon decided to test his new things on himself and had Medusa look right at him. And...

He didn't turn to stone.

Brindle could feel how happy Medusa was. Dragon called them all over.

"Take a look at our new friend, Medusa," the Dragon said with a tired voice.

Brindle and all her friends saw Medusa for the first time. She definitely had snakes for hair. And...

"You put sunglasses on all her snake eyes and her eyes as well... Ingenious!" exclaimed Savvy Skeleton.

"Now why didn't I think of that?" Zombie asked, admiring Dragon's work.

"She looks ridiculous. Glasses are ridiculous!" said Rat.

"I don't think she looks ridiculous," said Brindle. "I think she looks really beautiful with her new glasses."

Medusa looked at her new friends.

And she cried. But Brindle could tell that they were happy tears. Medusa could see them, and they could see her, and she was no longer alone.

"Thank you so much!"

Everyone was very happy for her.

"Well, Brindle," the Dragon waited until everyone's excitement for Medusa settled down. "There is something that I have wanted to do for a long, long, long time. And it may be a very difficult journey. I hate to cut the party short, but it is time for you to help me."

"I want a tea party," he finally announced.

Conclusion

The truth is, many things happen in our lives that we can tell stories about, and often times those stories can teach us enjoyable lessons!

Do you have any stories you can share that might have a valuable lesson that you can share with the people around you? If so, maybe you will consider writing your own bedtime story!

As you continue to help yourself fall asleep every night, I encourage you to make sure that you always maintain the best sleep routine possible.

Preparing your children for bed and winding down the same way every single night is a great way to let your body know it is time to sleep. Do you know why that is? The answer is: routine!

Moment by Moment, Ever-Changing

Mindfulness takes practice. You may need to work on it as you would any other skill.

A soccer player practices footwork. A dancer trains muscles. A mathematician solves problems step by step. You cannot master your mind without practicing MINDFUL ME skills every day.

Meditation is staying alert and resting your mind in its calm, relaxed, and natural state.

So, remember, mindfulness is a choice. Your choice. Being a MINDFUL ME is about connecting the dots between feeling an emotion, thinking a thought, and acting on them.

It is about using meditation to train your mind and expand your heart.

Be mindful NOW.

And NOW.

And NOW. Do your best in each moment. And thank yourself for being a MINDFUL

ME.

Your body and mind love having the same hints that it is time to do something like eat or go to sleep. When you take the time to make your sleep routine a habit, your body and mind begin to learn that this routine means it is time to go to sleep.

Soon, your body will automatically begin winding down and getting tired when you start the routine, even long before you actually finish it! This is the magic of your body and mind.

As you continue to repeat the habit and see these benefits, you will find yourself having a much better sleep every single night. Plus, it will become much easier for you to fall asleep because you are actually tired and ready for a good rest. This means that when waking up, you will be ready to enjoy plenty of great fun with your friends and family all over again!

Thank you, and I wish you many wonderful dreams. Goodnight!

CPSIA information can be obtained
at www.ICGtesting.com
Printed in the USA
BVHW061412250221
601119BV00001B/118